Parallels of Light

Parallels of Light

Written by

Wallace E. Martin

and

Jean Ann Shirey

Photographs

by

Wallace E. Martin

Parallels of Light

by Wallace E. Martin and Jean Ann Shirey

Photographs by Wallace E. Martin

Copyright 2019 Wallace E. Martin and Jean Ann Shirey

Lamb's Ear Publishing

ISBN: 9780615705484

Library of Congress Control Number:
2019902690

Abbreviations

AMP indicates the Amplified Bible.

NISB signifies the New Inductive Study Bible which is an updated edition of the New American Standard Bible.

KJV connotes the King James Version of the Bible.

ESV designates the English Standard Version of the Bible.

The photographs are sunrises, and no filters were used. The photograph on the cover and the other similar photos were taken in Texas about a week before Hurricane Ike in 2008.

Dedication

Parallels of Light is dedicated
to all who seek God.

To my sister, Jeanne, my consistent
source of kindness and love; a true follower
of Jesus, her light never fades.

Wallace E. Martin - WM

Wallace has delighted me with his
many talents and gifts. I acknowledge you,
dear brother, as a treasure from God while
praying the greatest blessings on you and
your family. I love you!

Jean Ann Shirey - JS

To the Reader

All that is around us on this earth is God's creation. To become in tune with God's word, is to have a better understanding of all. There are many parallels concerning people, creations and God. These teach harmony, peace, and love.

WM

"Parallels of Light" is the result of Wallace and I writing two works separately which fit together in order without modification. A poem I had already written was added, as well as a little for the book to complete my part. *This flow of harmony was a gift from God for you.*

JS

Acknowledgements

We would like to thank our God, who illuminates everything. We are sincerely grateful to our editors, Caitlin Smith and Sylvia Odenwald, for their invaluable assistance with *Parallels of Light.* Thank you, Nora Barnes, for this lovely book cover and Kim Giles, By Design, for your beautiful graphic design. The proofreaders are greatly appreciated for their contributions.

In Your light, we see light.

Psalm 36:9b NISB

Wallace E. Martin and Jean Ann Shirey

12 Then Jesus again spoke to them, saying, "I am the Light of the world; he who follows Me will not walk in the darkness, but will have the Light of life."

John 8:12 (NISB)

* * * * * * *

The morning sun comes in glory, breaking the darkness with rays of light. Jesus will be coming on the clouds with His radiant light.

WM

23 And the city has no need of sun or moon to shine on it, for the glory of God gives it light, and its lamp is the Lamb.

Revelation 21:23 (ESV)

* * * * * * *

When Jesus comes on the clouds, the entire world will see the light of The Lamb, The Lion of David. The Light that illuminates heaven will penetrate all of the air space and all of the ocean depths, the most glorious sunrise of all.

WM

5 And the Light shines on in the darkness, for the darkness has never overpowered it [put it out or absorbed it or appropriated it, and is unreceptive to it].

John 1:5 (AMP)

Threads of Light

I love the way

You light thoughts

with threads

of exposed form

in wondrous beauty,

showing life

in unexpected places,

moving me

with Your transparency.

You sing my soul

into Your love.

JS

1 In the beginning God created the heaven and the earth.

2 And the earth was without form, and void; and darkness *was* upon the face of the deep. And the Spirit of God moved upon the face of the waters.

3 And God said, Let there be light: and there was light.

Genesis 1:1-3 (KJV)

* * * * * * *

How great the Father is to create this essential source of life that parallels His creative, core teaching in the importance of light. There is physical light and spiritual light. When you see the sun rising, you are looking at light created by the supreme Light to mirror His wisdom without words.

WM

4 And God saw the light, that it was good: and God divided the light from the darkness.

Genesis 1:4 (KJV)

* * * * * * *

A key element to acquire understanding is the clear observation of all parts. Once again, God reflects His divine words through His creation. Darkness symbolizes man's ignorance of God's will and is associated with sin. Walk in the light, and seek God when it is dark. Look for light in all things you encounter.

WM

8 For you were formerly darkness, but now you are Light in the Lord; walk as children of Light.

Ephesians 5:8 (NISB)

Shadows

Your light also

shows shadows,

where forms

move away

from You.

Your being

distinguishes all.

You ignite

fires

of discernment

within me.

JS

4 In Him was life, and the life was the Light of men.

John 1:4 (NISB)

* * * * * * *

God is illuminated Holiness. Jesus is so divine, His presence radiates Light. We can hardly comprehend this wisdom, but we can see it on the water and in the clouds. His creation speaks to all who listen and watch.

WM

35 So Jesus said to them, You will have the Light only a little while longer. Walk while you have the Light [keep on living by it], so that darkness may not overtake and overcome you. He who walks about in the dark does not know where he goes [he is drifting].

John 12:35 (AMP)

* * * * * * *

Jesus is the Truth. He is "the bright and Morning Star."[1] Set your thoughts and your eyes on the true Light. He is talking to us and explaining Himself through His creations.

WM

[1]Revelation 22:16 (KJV)

25 And in the fourth watch of the night he came to them, walking on the sea.

26 When the disciples saw him walking on the sea, they were terrified, and said, "It is a ghost!" and they cried out in fear.

27 But immediately Jesus spoke to them, saying, "Take heart; it is I. Do not be afraid."

Matthew 14:25-27 (ESV)

Reflection

Reflection of Your love

brought to me,

for me to be

the reflection of Your love

to those I see

while You reflected

God to me.

Love's own You are,

the embodiment of Light,

and I bask in Your glory.

JS

39 And he arose, and rebuked the wind, and said unto the sea, Peace, be still. And the wind ceased, and there was a great calm.

Mark 4:39 (KJV)

39 And He arose and rebuked the wind and said to the sea, Hush now! Be still (muzzled)! And the wind ceased (sank to rest as if exhausted by its beating) and there was [immediately] a great calm (a perfect peacefulness).

Mark 4:39 (AMP)

39 And He got up and rebuked the wind and said to the sea, "Hush, be still." And the wind died down and it became perfectly calm.

Mark 4:39 (NISB)

The oceans know the authority of God for He created them. God has authority over the sun for He created it. They merge in testimony of His glory every sunrise and sunset.

WM

105 Your word is a lamp to My feet and a
light to my path.

Psalm 119:105 (ESV)

12 For the word of God is living and active and sharper than any two-edged sword, and piercing as far as the division of soul and spirit, of both joints and marrow, and able to judge the thoughts and intentions of the heart.

Hebrews 4:12 (NISB)

The Transformation

I walked outside the store

and stood transfixed.

You painted the largest canvas

I had ever seen,

and I was mesmerized.

You literally caressed the left,

and it took my breath to see it

like the moment of first touch.

You blew your breath

on lines, themes, and variations

of hues and contrasts.

I could not move.

I felt stirrings in me of love

as if I never knew You before –

not really.

I went everywhere,

looking, hearing, feeling,

and then You changed the light.

It was almost more

then I could bear.

It overflowed and overwhelmed me.

I couldn't breathe or blink

wanting to see all.

I came to – walked. It faded.

My heart beat again,

but altered.

JS

11 And have no fellowship with the unfruitful works of darkness, but rather reprove *them*.

Ephesians 5:11 (KJV)

* * * * * * *

Consider the sun and the Son. Without light, we perish in both cases. There is an unimaginable creation in the sun, an internal fire of unfathomable intensity. God created man in His image. He gave us light as a reminder of the power of God and our need to seek wisdom through the light of Jesus.

WM

11 For the sun rises with its scorching heat and withers the grass; its flower falls, and its beauty perishes. So also will the rich man fade away in the midst of his pursuits.

James 1:11 (ESV)

4 And coming to Him as to a living stone which has been rejected by men, but is choice and precious in the sight of God.

1Peter 2:4 (NISB)

Parallels of light are apparent daily. Light can bring forth life, and it can bring forth death. The wisdom of the Lord and the ways of the world are different. The light of the Lord brings forth true peace. There is no light in the world without Jesus. The sunlight comes and goes, but the light of the Lord sustains spiritual and eternal life, filling our cup with Holy wisdom and mercy.

WM

19 "This is the judgment, that the Light has come into the world, and men loved the darkness rather than the Light, for their deeds were evil."

John 3:19 (NISB)

Prayer for a Relationship with God

Have mercy on me, O God,

for You and You alone can save me.

You acted properly toward me.

I sinned against You.

You loved me to the death

of Your Son, Jesus.

Please forgive me, receive me,

change me, and let me live for You.

I receive Your love, Your Light.

Help me to shine for You.

I know Jesus lives as my Savior!

In the name of the Father, the Son

and the Holy Spirit, I pray.

Amen

JS

17 Every good gift and every perfect gift is from above, coming down from the Father of lights with whom there is no variation or shadow due to change.

James 1:17 (ESV)

* * * * * * *

Jesus said, "Peace, be still"[2] to the sea. He said, "Be of good cheer; it is I; be not afraid"[3] to His disciples. The supreme authority is Love: pure, uncompromised, divine wisdom. He loves us who believe.

WM

[2]Mark 4:39 (KJV)
[3]Matthew 14:27b (KJV)

16 "Let your light shine before men in such a way that they may see your good works, and glorify your Father who is in heaven."

Matthew 5:16 (NISB)

13 So now faith, hope, and love abide, these three; but the greatest of these is love.

1 Corinthians 13:13 (ESV)

Hand Up

Delicate joy,

sprinkled grace,

stirred love,

reaching for hands to lift,

higher calling.

Come,

come to Jesus.

Here is my hand. Come.

The Light gives

clean hands and pure hearts.

Come walk with me to Jesus!

JS

45 So that you may be sons of your Father who is in heaven. For he makes his sun rise on the evil and on the good, and sends rain on the just and on the unjust.

Matthew 5:45 (ESV)

Jesus confirms the light of His Father's sun and the Light of His Son are parallel. The light of the sun leaves us no choice, but heavenly Light is a personal choice. Choose wisely the light of your path.

Jesus reminds us of the power and authority of God. "He causes His sun to rise..." Matthew 5:45b, (NISB). Listen to what He is saying. The sun is a gift for physical life on earth. The Light of the Lord allows equalization for man. It allows us to choose, to believe or not. "But blessed are your eyes, because they see; and your ears, because they hear." (Matthew 13:16, NISB). Jesus said those who believe are blessed.

WM

Fire of Light and Life comes to the one who loves Jesus. Being joined to Christ Jesus is an amazing experience of Light, a union with Light. Nothing is ever the same. The Light is present with the believer, and surrender to Jesus brings an incredible, indescribable, miraculous oneness with the God of the universe. This unfolds in the core of each human being who chooses to follow the Light.

JS

29 When Moses came down from Mount Sinai with the two tablets of the testimony in his hand as he came down from the mountain, Moses did not know that the skin of his face shone because he had been talking with God.

Exodus 34:29 (ESV)

17 And after six days Jesus took with him Peter and James, and John his brother, and led them up a high mountain by themselves.

2 And he was transfigured before them, and his face shone like the sun, and his clothes became white as light.

Matthew 17:1- 2 (ESV)

* * * * * *

The light of the sun is too intense to be stared upon and can cause burns. The Light, Jesus, has infinite riches of light, and He constantly reveals Himself to His believers.

WM & JS

12 Then Jesus again spoke to them, saying, "I am the Light of the world; he who follows Me will not walk in the darkness, but will have the Light of life."

John 8:12 (NISB)

17 Therefore if anyone is in Christ, he is a new creation. The old has passed away; behold, the new has come.

2 Corinthians 5:17 (ESV)

3 Now as he went on his way, he approached Damascus, and suddenly a light from heaven shone around him.

4 And falling to the ground he heard a voice saying to him, "Saul, Saul, why are you persecuting me?"

5 And he said, "Who are you, Lord?" And he said, "I am Jesus, whom you are persecuting."

Acts 9:3-5 (ESV)

3 When His lamp shone over my head, *And* by His light I walked through darkness;

Job 29:3 (NISB)

BEHOLD, HE IS COMING WITH THE CLOUDS, and every eye will see Him, even those who pierced Him; and all the tribes of the earth will mourn over Him. So it is to be.

Amen.

Revelation 1:7 (NISB)

* * * * * * *

Be in anticipation of His glorious return with a personal rebirth or born again spirit. Be of good cheer and turn from old ways. The Holy Light of Jesus will be visible to all, and all will know.

WM

3 Jesus answered him, "Truly, truly, I say to you, unless one is born again he cannot see the kingdom of God."

John 3:3 (ESV)

* * * * * * *

The sun comes and comes again. The Son of God, Jesus the Christ, came, and He will come again.

JS

18 … I died, and behold, I am alive

forever more, and I have the keys of

Death and Hades.

Revelation 1:18b (ESV)

9 There was the true Light which, coming

into the world, enlightens every man.

John 1:9 (NISB)

My Door, I Adore

My door, my way, my maker:

You light my path with glory,

wipe away my tears,

and bring me joy.

I am on this earth,

made of clay,

but You give me light

to find You clearly.

You let me see the way

to You, my door,

and to all beyond.

You opened me

to Your love and light.

God of Love, I adore You.

18 "And to the angel of the church in Thyatira write:
'The words of the Son of God, who has eyes like a flame of fire, and whose feet are like burnished bronze.'

Revelation 2:18 (ESV)

* * * * * * *

Jesus' light cannot be contained. It is hard to comprehend such Holiness, but *He loves you*. Watch with faith, hope with cheer, and listen with patience.

WM

* * * * * * *

2 Continue steadfastly in prayer, being watchful in it with thanksgiving.

Colossians 4:2 (ESV)

79 To give light to them that sit in darkness and in the shadow of death, to guide our feet into the way of peace.

Luke 1:79 (KJV)

* * * * * * *

Jesus, Light, is hope. Holy Light is the tenderest hand when there is none. The Comforter is peace, and He brings forth opportunity for eternal life without tears, pain or sorrow.

WM

* * * * * * *

4 And God shall wipe away all tears from their eyes; and there shall be no more death, neither sorrow, nor crying, neither shall there be any more pain: for the former things are passed away.

Revelation 21:4 (KJV)

2 The people who walked in darkness have seen a great light; those who dwelt in a land of deep darkness, on them has light shone.

Isaiah 9:2 (ESV)

2 And behold, the glory of the God of Israel was coming from the east. And the sound of his coming was like the sound of many waters, and the earth shone with His glory.

Ezekiel 43:2 (ESV)

GLORY!

Ohhhhhhh, GLORY!

Praise to the LORD "WHO WAS AND WHO

IS AND WHO IS TO COME."[4]

I chase the sun with You

each day as the evening sets,

and the Son greets me again

at first rise morning glance.

My friend, joy and hope,

I live[A] You, and You light me with Glory!

JS

[4] Revelation 4:8b (NISB)
[A] live-- to remain alive

2 [But] in the last of these days He has spoken to us in [the person of a] Son, Whom He appointed Heir and lawful Owner of all things, also by and through Whom He created the worlds and the reaches of space and the ages of time [He made, produced, built, operated, and arranged them in order].

3 He is the sole expression of the glory of God [the Light-being, the out-raying or radiance of the divine], and He is the perfect imprint and very image of [God's] nature, upholding and maintaining and guiding and propelling the universe by His mighty word of power. When He had by offering Himself accomplished our cleansing of sins and riddance of guilt, He sat down at the right hand of the divine Majesty on high,

Hebrews 1:2-3 (AMP)

In His hands are the keys to life and to death. The Light of the Lord shines the way of salvation – peace. Jesus is the Light for man, and He wants to be the Light for you to bring you home.

WM

9 Do not grumble against one another, brothers, so that you may not be judged; behold, the Judge is standing at the door.

James 5:9 (ESV)

Light's Lead

You led me in ways

known to You,

unseen by me.

You whisper

with Your song,

near to me

as You are always,

and I follow You.

Light form,

teacher of trust,

ever doing good

to me and others.

You light life

by a moment's leading

to directions

I would never guess,

and I love You more

for knowing.

JS

The Testimony

See the sun?

God sent the Son for you and me.

Sunset, then darkness overtakes you?

The Son died for us.

Brilliant sunrise,

the Son rose from the dead!

The sun comes back again?

The Son will return!

See the sun?

Notice the testimony.

Testify sun! Testify!

Jesus is the Son of God!

Sun in your face, surrounding you?

Jesus' love is near,

personal and true.

Witness bold and strong,

quiet, present reminder,

sun to Son,

Jesus is the promise,

the Messiah.

Return the Son!

JS

12 Then Jesus again spoke to them, saying, "I am the Light of the world; he who follows Me will not walk in the darkness, but will have the Light of life."

John 8:12 (NISB)

Footnotes

1) I, Jesus, have sent mine angel to testify unto you these things in the churches. I am the root and the offspring of David, and the bright and morning star.

Revelation 22:16 (KJV)

2) Peace, be still.

Mark 4:39b (KJV)

3) Be of good cheer; it is I: be not afraid.

Matthew 14:27b (KJV)

4) "HOLY, HOLY, HOLY IS THE LORD GOD, THE ALMIGHTY, WHO WAS AND WHO IS AND WHO IS TO COME."

Revelation. 4:8 b (NISB)

ABOUT THE AUTHORS

WALLACE E. MARTIN
Author and Photographer

WALLACE E. MARTIN states: "My eyes are fixed toward Him who is coming on the clouds, and I am awaiting the trumpet sounds." Wallace lives near the coastal waters of Texas with his family.

"My sister, Jean Ann, and I are not only siblings, but we are kindred spirits through the Holy Spirit. We have never had a cross word."

JEAN ANN SHIREY
Poetess

JEAN ANN SHIREY graduated from Baylor University. She worked in the Texas Department of Criminal Justice Institutional Division for 22 years and for the University of Texas Medical Branch—Institutional Division many of those years. Jean Ann has four married children and eighteen grandchildren. Jean Ann Shirey also wrote *Plum Delight: Poetry of the Earth*, *The Dance of Monterrey*, *White Hall Baptist Church: The Little Country Church of Your Dreams*, *Trumpet Cloud: Poems Of Jesus*, *Dear God, Granny's Garden*, and *Honeymoon in Hawaii.*

"Wallace and I have always enjoyed being together, and collaborating on this book is the fruit of God's generosity. Wallace's writing and photographs remind me of God's particular, loving care."